The Word According to Crow

Sinéad McClure

Winner of the Roscommon Chapbook Bursary Award 2022

**Comhairle Contae
Ros Comáin**
Roscommon
County Council

THE CALENDAR ROAD PRESS

Go n-éirí an bóthar leat

Contents

The Word According to Crow *1*
Stifle *2*
A pangolin speaks *3*
How the jackdaw sees angelica *4*
Faltering *5*
The Padre and the plantation *6*
To those who know the ending *7*
Somewhere, in the long grass, a pygmy shrew
is contemplating life *9*
Preparing my dog for reincarnation *10*
"There is no peace" says your God "for the wicked." *11*
In Nagoro Village scarecrows outnumber people ten-to-one *13*
On the anatomy of birds *14*
The Clockmaker *15*
A walk in the country *16*
Hedgerow *17*
You fell asleep listening to Gabriel Faurés Pavane *18*
My brother the orangutan *19*
A rook longs for a badger *20*
Fox *21*
There *23*
Curlew Logic *24*
Hawk *25*
Moths *27*
Dream Catcher *28*

*"There's a void in the forest
where the trees failed to prosper.
A small clearing.
This is where I genuflect."*

The Word According to Crow

Rooks do good mimicry but this orator is no priest,
collarless and open-beaked he shifts his weight on the steeple.
His sermon, a daily litany of caws and trills.

Nearby a swallow threeps thoughts on Africa;
fears of the journey, the hot flight across the Sahara.
She asks for blessings turning north, the rook ignores her.

He waits for his brothers' responses;

The raven in the mountain.
I am here

The orange-beaked chough by the sea.
I am here

The hoodie on the high wire.
I am here

The jackdaw waving from the chimney.
I am here

The jay half-dressed in electric blue.
I am here

Above them, a kestrel circles,
writes today's first catch
wing to cloud. *One for sorrow.*

A black and white streak of cirrus-crow
evaporates to silence.

Stifle

Where does Keshcorran go in the fog?
Does it leave the Bricklieves,
tiptoe towards the Ox?
Or maybe strike out further still
to the Atlantic, to thrill in its surf.

Sometimes fog can linger for days.
Enough time for this hill
to make it all the way to Iceland,
speak with volcanoes.

Next time someone
sets fire to the whin,
blazes out the nesting birds,
skims grass back
to bare rock

this silent hill
may have learned
how to blow its top.

A pangolin speaks

We are the most trafficked animal in the world,
always taken, left in dark spaces.

Our scales crow;
Oh to be someone's remedy
Oh to be mined like diamonds!

They slice trees around us,
our hollowed-out homes
just big enough
for our hard bodies.
There are other chasms
we don't want to climb into.

An errant bone may choke you
or at least make you cough.
Feel the copper of our tongues
lick silence lung-ward.

We sleep in what trees are left standing.
Lay our eggs deep.
Wait for the axe.

Wish our scales were nettles
Wish our scales were daggers
Wish our scales were ours.

How the jackdaw sees angelica

She stands, arms out, open-palmed.
Her white umbels grab leafhoppers in flight.
They delicately bite at her scent.
Soon she is standing everywhere, as towers

or hoisted umbrellas, keeping seeds for bullfinches
to nibble on and shade for shrews to sleep beneath.

She is taller than people. I envy the curve
of her slender body, and how it seems
she's always dancing even in the rain.

Faltering

I ask the wasp to hold one end of this poem
for he is here with me now in this crow of November,

yellow jacket fraying at the edges. I sit with my back to the alder,
the hoodie wants to be a lyrebird in summer

he cries out of the air, dry as hot parchment
I close my eyes and I can feel the world

has hit its tipping point, a globe rolling to a stop.
Soon the wind will pick itself up from the sycamore ground,

dial itself in revolutions, until it finds the winter
and drops it upon me, unannounced. The wasp will let go.

The Padre and the plantation
For Jho

I'll tie him to a tree
you answered when the woman
in the gift shop in Knock
asked where you'd place his graven image

her face spoke tongues of bemusement
as we left laughing, the Padre wrapped
in brown paper, tucked under your arm.
He *was* your mother's favourite.

Lichen touches everything up here.
The dry stone wall jig-sawed together,
a puzzle nearly lost beneath the cloth of algae
and the thick air of evergreen plantation.

Padre Pio never did get tied to the tree.
When you started to get better
he became sainted on the best shelf
with a view overlooking the garden.

There's a void in the forest
where the trees failed to prosper.
A small clearing.
This is where I genuflect.

To those who know the ending

I write murder mysteries while I walk.
Today the perpetrator is the tall thin man
in the black gabardine who crosses to stop
in my path, terrier pointing ditch-ward.

I move quick, refuse to look behind.
He doesn't know I'm on to him,
the bystander, the witness
who'll create his perfect photo-fit,
the arched expression,
those rookish shoulders,
that syphilitic nose.

One day I wrote the story of the missing jogger.
The lady lapped me on my circular walk.
Road, forest, road,
forest, road.

Gone.

Taken on the quietest part
where the trees touch.

The false alarms,
the car that slowed, turned, sped away.
The man who would be Stephen King,
if not lost in my rural spot,
caught me up,
passed me by.

Most readers of my mysteries wonder why
these are unsolvable crimes?
Why nobody remembers anything?
Why no clues are left behind?
I try to resolve this on shorter walks,
end up in circles, again.

There is no conclusion, just a constant
re-working of scenario, unknown antagonists,
and a plea to the orbital characters
who always know something, to speak

the gnawing in the pit of your stomach,
the bit that grates when you see another appeal,
the story that waits for your death bed confession,
the secrets *you* take when you walk.

Somewhere, in the long grass,
a pygmy shrew is contemplating life.

And she is hiding out here
grateful for the respite
of a short attention span.
Nibbling a woodlouse
she wonders how much more she'll have to eat
to stay alive today,
more than her bodyweight again?
Maybe she'll stride out purposefully
give herself up to the hawk
or raise a tiny fist at an owl.
She stares at the Heberden's nodes
standing out on her knuckles
—even rodents get arthritis
in the mid-months of their life.
She knows she's just a speck
on her patch of grass
thinks fleetingly beyond this field
where terror lives.
Sounds, and sights not meant for shrews.
Dreams fly her there
and nightmares bring her back.
Hot and then cold.
A memory of the autumn rain
beating sharply against
her naked children
as she caravans them to safety, tail to teeth.
A feat carried out less these days
as each slow second passes.

Preparing my dog for reincarnation

I give you cooking tips
you watch on,
tilt your head
try to understand

Be patient for the rise
or
a couple of anchovies add flavour.

Loaves and then fishes.

I tell you to assert yourself
speak your mind
don't sit in the corner
don't do the canine things
don't be fox or wolf
own your place in the world.

I lose you to the swinging door,
the evening sunshine,
to Russian Roulette with the wasps,

to this dog's life.
No care or thought
for any other moment.

"There is no peace," says your God, "for the wicked."

I had no choice but to pass by the church
when its loudspeaker cut the damp air of a soft Irish day.

Take this all of you

Even head phoned with Ripperton—
singing about simpler things—
I could not quieten the testament;

This is my body

As I walked on, the words faded behind me
absorbed in the caws of a crow morning.
But the anger stayed, it followed me, a ruffle at first,
like ripples on the swelling river, lapping heavily
against the bank where tiny fish hang
in the shadows hoping not to be seen.

Anger escorted me across the bridge
and wound along uphill. Getting out of breath
it fell behind for a short while before catching up,
it chased every country bend until it stood beside me,
and in the wide view of the valley opening out below,
anger became rage, and each step I took towards that church
was marked with my defiance.

I don't need to hear sermons or testaments,
or witness sacraments.
I want to walk on unconsecrated ground,
these are the richest of all places, unsullied by religion.

Where worms languish in darkness,
make mulch for beetles and their larvae.
Where insects play unabashed in the detritus.
So much manure, and muck.

I would welcome that lively murk
compared to the paradise your loudspeaker spits.

Sleep in its loam, allow the birds to peck.
Eventually all shapes, and colours
are winged away in beak and talon.

Know that
one day
tiny bones
will drop from high,
and rain upon the culpable
in a silent, unceasing storm.

In Nagoro village, scarecrows outnumber people
ten-to-one.

My father yearned for deserted islands.
People grow better in silence, music will follow.
He retreated from our world, climbed into Verdi
mouthing *Woman is flighty*.

Oh and yes we were wayward, cut from him,
and he was King among us.

As I age to pass his middle years
I crave a silence where music should grow.
Hear it out here among the trees, feel it cling
the way fruticose takes to branches.

I allow the hush to thread itself
along the outline of my shadow
tack in at the shoulders, latch the dark
and hold me together in its lockstitch.

In Nagoro village scarecrows outnumber people ten-to-one.
When they leave they are replaced by ragdolls.
A scarecrow gardener, farmer, flower seller,
an entire school of scarechicks in effigy reminders.

Aughris Village was a once busy clochán,
no longer any blacksmiths, no dressmakers,
no publicans, no teachers, no tailors,
no shopkeepers, no carpenters, no bootmakers,
not even a washerwoman.

Still, the ocean feeds its solid walls
with defiant music, and I cling on,
straw falling out at my feet.

On the anatomy of birds

We could be birds; femurs, vertebrae, kneecaps
not for kneeling on— funny bones.

Sometimes noble with our crowns and our crests,
throats sore from shaping song instead of speech.

Bellies full. Bellies emptied. Bent at the scapula
only in the rain. Warm blood does not make a mammal.

Birds could just as easily be boats, high keels
and a trailing-edge-of-underwing

touching the half-frozen water
as colourful sails, ice split in those splashes.

Birds are a puzzle, an abacus of digits at their wingtips,
feet and feathers, hallux and coverts.

In Florida, a Baltimore oriole eats grape jelly
and fresh oranges as bright as his breast.

In Australia, a lyrebird mimics the sound of chainsaws
to impress his mate.

In my garden, a robin pretends to be a dead relative
in exchange for mealworms.

The Clockmaker

The balance wheel has shifted.
He focuses one eye on escape.
The innards are slowly winding down—
ratchets, plates and barrels
— a spine clicks, a bird wakes
with head pain again.

Ignorance is emptying
across tilled fields,
in the straightening cogs,
and the loosening of habitat.
A once-tight collet.

He blinks and a tear
begins to fall.
Here it's a shower,
over there
a deluge
and even further
islands disappear beneath
the exit pallet.

The ribcage of earth opened,
the mechanism steaming-gold
and hot-white light.
Tiny jewels rise to the surface.

All we have is a fading beat
the forced opening of a 500-year-old mollusc
failing to snap shut, running out of time.

A walk in the country

is pot-holed tarmac
soft at its edges
birds pass notes in song
add wings to my shadow
hills nod familiarly
the smell of silage
freshly opened
a dead calf

a dead calf
at her mother's feet
I ask is she okay?
the cow prods her
no
she will not leave her
the vet and farmer drive away
allow her time with her sisters
and their lively calves
let them wake this loss

I round each tight bend
beneath the daggered branches of blackthorn
the road, at last, turns downward
to the forest and refuge
in the distance the cries of a keening mother

Hedgerow

Each part of me is hedgerow,
blackthorn blooms early on this twig.

A dog rose at my cupid's bow
and hazelnuts caught loosely in my teeth.
I winter with snowberries and cuckoo-pint.
Silently squash myself beneath frosted angelica
where holly   breaks   my skin.

Each part of me is part of here—
a bramble jigsaw.   This is where
the birds fall   into open hands.
Each nest for the cupping.

When you rip out hedgerow, you scalp at my feet,
you topple me and all that I keep,
each breath of bird, and vein of leaf
in swift replete.
I will spill seeds   first as stars
then as bombs,
quietly, detonating.

Implore stitchwort
to tack the hem of me
to earth   and wait.

You fell asleep listening to Gabriel Fauré's Pavane

Grass moves in June as music in F-sharp minor,
breath of bow teasing violin, backwards then forwards.

A birdhouse full of busy chicks hits the ground
loud enough to silence it.

The same motion steals young apples from the orchard.
Little winged fruits flying before the windfall.

Leaves a shiver in the trees, breaks the ash branches
into wishbones.

I thought you'd freeze to death out here,
a thin blanket tucking you in between sky and floor.

I hear you cough awake, rasp the evening out
like a great tit, calling for her dead children.

My brother, the orangutan

When I left the forest
I left my brother behind
But he didn't mind

He liked the way the trees spread upwards to the sky
They travel up, so high
he'd say.

You'd often find him there
Hugging the stars
His furry shadow embossed by their light
Right up there, he was.

It was here he slept
His hammock
an intricate nest in the curve
where branch met trunk.

He told me he kissed the trees
Thank them for keeping me safe
he'd say
They are my sky
They are my home
They are my larder
As the soft fruit spilled from his lips

When we came back to the forest
we forgot our brother, the orangutan.
We cut his house
We took his food
We left him too far from his sky.

And the soft fruit spilled from my lips
he said

A rook longs for a badger

Where did the badgers go?
We miss their cuts—
the cold wheels rut in snow
the nose-sized pockets—
knit these fields for years.

Now we must peck deeper
for our worms
through new wet grass
frosted in ice
our feathers liquorice-black
in the slick soft Irish winter.

Rook calls;

Don't cull
all should be full
for nature to persevere.

Cull
and fall
towards a constant winter.

Fox

Each night we feed them dry kibble
frozen in blocks big enough to fit the jaw
even though we saw
what they did here,
how they silently attacked the muscovies
ribbon-red on icy days.
How they gathered in groups
to take the chickens.
Carried them away without leaving a feather.

When we stopped keeping poultry
they still called around
waited by the back door
orange tails tickling the concrete
until we gifted a salmon head,
a chicken leg, a piece of bread
and now every evening after
they are fed a complete mix
to keep their red coats shiny.

They don't trust us,
approach in parcels,
one keeps watch
as the others wind their way
through the long grass.

They still know fox haters,
corrugated people
who carry shotguns
when sheep are yeaning.
Set traps deep in the forest
with teeth sharper
than any creature's bite.

A fox cry up here
strikes fault lines through the mist
leaves an echo hanging in the hollows.
A deep wound
we dress each day,
until it heals.

There

After Early One Summer by W.S Merwin

It is spring equinox
soon a metal mast will grow
out of the boglands
and all that flies
will stop falling

This is why the millipedes are testing
a new communication system
on our back wall

All feet cling
to the concrete
slender bodies tick

tell me
it's already five to midnight
and moths will steal the dark

Curlew Logic

I'm a curlew
With my cew, cew
cur—lee—cur—lee
whistle

and my long legs
and cur—vey beak

I'm a curlew
That's me
behind the thistle,
looking dappled
and rather sleek

I'm a curlew
With my cew, cew
cur—lee—cur—lee
whistle

And my currycomb
shaped eyes

I'm a curlew
a cursed curlew
With a curvilinear
point of view

curt but cautious
with my curlicue beak

I'm a curlew
don't forget me
If it's curiosity you seek.

Hawk

Walking the long acre
the clamped-shut quiet of August
is interrupted by a clatter in the sycamore.
A flurry of calls;

Alert! Alert! Alert!

Siskins scream, one of their own is taken.

I see it happen right in front of me.
A tiny bird dangles in talons.
A hawk sweeps through the trees,
leaving feathers and leaves to fall.

It happens so swiftly, almost as if it didn't happen at all.
Yet here in this wild acre it probably happens every day.

Each morning siskins prepare for attack
tell each other not to fly too high,
perch too long, practice
how not to be birds.

Somewhere, far from here
women prepare for attack,
gather each morning,
tell each other what to wear,

where to be safe, practice
how not to be women.

Still, he will swoop in, carry her away in his talons.

The hawk returns to the long acre,
hangs high
patient for a catch,
beak dry
thin belly
empty.

Soft feathers settle
on the air,
the sycamore leaves continue to fall.

Moths

You won't remember this;
They will show you pictures,

ask you questions,
talk to you as they would a child.

It will be as if the window
of summer has firmly closed

and the moths, the ermine and the burnet
hang from webs at its edges.

But moths will find a way inside your brain.
A map-winged swift will take new strands,

hot electric rods to strike against each other.
More will come, flutter by tiny beacons as each is relit.

The common lutestring will remember music,
the lesser yellow underwing will take you under his.

Finally, the drinker moth will sip you in.
And a window will open, again.

Dream Catcher

The day you moved the dream catcher
from the shed it had hung in for twenty years

I knew we were letting go of ourselves.
Wild things took over. Fields filled up easily.

Buttercups in May, meadowsweet in July,
purple-headed self-heal a mat beneath the apple trees.

When I threw out the dying chrysanthemums
one clung to the nettle bed still breathing,
and the forest became itself again.

Now there is a cadence to our steps
and joined-up writing in the sky
as we traipse the sun and its long-shadow paths.

The dream catcher takes our harshest winters
holds tight, to spin forever from the alder.

Acknowledgements

The following poems, or versions of them, have been previously published; *Faltering* At the Edge of all Storms Dreich, *Somewhere, in the long grass, a pygmy shrew is contemplating life* Not the Time to be Silent Collected Works *"There is no peace" said your God, "for the wicked."* & *Hawk* A New Ulster, *Fox* Live Encounters Poetry & Writing, *Curlew Logic*, Drawn to the Light Press, *Dream Catcher* Southword Autumn/Winter Edition 2022. Thanks to Orla Fay, Siobhan Potter, Patrick Cotter, Jack Carodoc, Amos Grieg and Mark Ulyseas. Warm thanks and appreciation to all the editors who shine a light on and strive to share the written word.

The poem *On the anatomy of birds* won first prize at the Cathal Buí Hedge School, Belcoo, 2022. The poem *A rook longs for a badger* won first prize in the Ó Bhéal Five Word International Poetry Prize, 2021.

Writing can be a solitary pursuit but I'm delighted to know a collaborative community of poets, and to call them my friends; Thanks to Terry McDonagh for being a mentor and a constant support, to Cáit O'Neill McCullagh my sister poet, to Maeve McKenna my companion on many a poetry filled walk and to Jan Claire Starkey for generously sharing her knowledge of the craft. Lime Square Poets and all their contributors for giving my work a space to be heard.

To the people who can be found in the spaces between the words, and regularly get subjected to my poetry, Alison Flynn, Mary McCallig, John McClure and Dee Hennessy and to my husband Jho Harris who is a constant support, even if he inhales sharply when I say "Can I read you a poem?" I love you dearly.

Thanks to Roscommon County Council for their dedication to the arts and to Lani O Hanlon for seeing what she saw in these pages.

Author Biography

"Writing the world I inhabit is very important to me. Conservation and preserving our natural habitat has been a strong feature in my work for many years, and I have felt that I am now engaging with place, and the beats of nature more than ever before." - Sinéad McClure

Sinéad 's work is published digitally, in print and on radio. You will find her poetry in The Stinging Fly, Live Encounters Poetry & Writing, Poethead, Southword, StepAway Magazine, and in many other fine publications.

Sinéad is also a writer for children and has written 15 radio dramas dealing with Ireland's natural heritage and conservation issues broadcast on RTEjr radio between 2009-2020.

Sinéad was the 2022 winner of the Cathal Buí Poetry Competion. Her collaborative chapbook written with Scottish poet Cáit O'Neill McCullagh "The songs I sing are sisters" is published by Dreich Press.

For more visit www.sineadmcclure.com

www.thecalendarroad.com

Made in United States
North Haven, CT
08 November 2022

26367245R00024